Essential Reverie

Essential Reverie

Vol. I

Steven Matusic

Himoniá Publishing House
Albuquerque, New Mexico

HIMONIA

Himoniá Publishing House
Albuquerque, NM

Cover art and design by Eli Maravich

ISBN 979-8-9883246-0-7 (paperback)
ISBN 979-8-9883246-1-4 (ebook)

First Himoniá Publishing House edition June 2023

Published by Himoniá Publishing House LLC
Albuquerque, NM
www.himoniabooks.com
inquiries@himoniabooks.com

Ad majorem Dei gloriam

Contents

A Note to the Reader: On Reverie

> Wonder is the feeling of a philosopher,
> and philosophy begins in wonder
> —Socrates

IN REVERIE THERE IS REVERENCE. Reverie by its very nature requires such reverence for the gift of life that one is held in awe, in perpetual wonder about what else might be learned of it.

Defined in dictionaries as daydreaming and fanciful musings, "reverie" has often been used as a way of calling something naïve or unsophisticated. Yet many great writers, thinkers, and wise men from all walks of life have understood that the most profound insights often come when we go for a walk, when we allow our minds to mosey about and wander off in wonder. This book, much like Rousseau's *Reveries of the Solitary Walker,* is a testament to the fruit of reverie—a thinking that remains in awe of life, that reveres all that has been given enough to be humble and excited in its exploration.

Essential Reverie

Quiet Moments, Quiet Thoughts

OUT AND ABOUT IN A BUSTLING WORLD, quiet circumstances are hard to come by. Even so, when quiet moments do arise, common practice is to quickly fill them with this or that flavor of distraction. While people do simply enjoy listening to music and indulging in various other forms of entertainment, is there perhaps another reason behind this common practice of filling up quiet moments with some sort of noise?

Indeed, it is not unheard of for quiet moments to be encountered as themselves *disquieting* or frightening: "alone with one's thoughts" the foreboding saying goes. If one's thoughts come to the fore in quiet moments, the implication is that one's thoughts are thus *themselves quieted* by the sounds of a bustling world or blaring ear-buds. The often very faint sound of our thoughts can be easily drowned out.

1

When the world around us is quiet, how-ever, what has been faintly present all along comes into focus. Good or bad, when we find ourselves in some quiet place without distrac-tion, we can thus find ourselves alone with our thoughts. If this frightens us, there is one last line of defense: to talk rather than listen. Just as two people cannot talk to each other at the same time, thinking is a discourse that requires silence.

If we seek a quiet moment—"a moment to think"—the quietude is necessary because we have to be able to hear the thoughts that come to us. First we quiet the world by turning off the television or we seek out some quiet oasis, but then we must also quiet ourselves. Thinking as an undertaking begins with the holding up of a question. "Questioning," Heidegger tells us, "is the piety of thought," and as Plato famously re-counted Socrates saying, "philosophy begins in wonder." But what does it mean to quiet our-selves, and how does such quieting relate to questioning and wonder?

Before we can wonder about something, we must give up the idea that we already fully grasp or understand completely what it is we intend to wonder about. Genuine questioning is an acknowledgment that various things remain yet unknown to us—it is an excited and hopeful inquiry into a matter of mystery and intrigue. In wonder we pose questions, and in quiet moments of questioning and wonder, it is possible for insight and wisdom to gracefully descend upon us.

Without assuming we already know the answers, however obvious they may seem, we humbly ask a question in a mood of wonder and thus allow our mind to wander, unsure of what it may find. Quiet thoughts come like loose threads of a warm sweater that never fully unravels, and we pull on those threads and see where they lead, often finding further questions, most fruitful questions, to wonder about.

A Day

WE ARE TOLD THAT A DAY IS 24 HOURS. People—in order to "make the most of their time"—plan their days and schedule various things according to measurements and calculations of minutes and hours: a walk between two places is so many minutes long; an hour's break between obligations will allow for roughly thirty minutes to eat lunch after travel time is taken into account; when working late into the evening, the hours previously allotted for sleep are cut into, etc. Because "there aren't enough hours in the day," what cannot be fit into one's schedule today or this week is slotted into an available hour belonging to tomorrow or next week. One 24-hour period appears the same as any other, and any rare exception to this general principle is itself noted and planned for in advance (e.g., holidays, if treated as such and duly celebrated, are planned and accounted for in the schedule ahead-of-time). The day thus repre-sented makes days by and large interchangeable and planning practices reflect this.

Viewed as such, it is common that the day's hours are carefully organized and used most efficiently in order to extract from each day the most productivity possible. Back roads and alternate routes are thus seen as viable *not* because they are more leisurely and manifest the beauty belonging to each season, but be-cause they might be more time-efficient than sitting in traffic. A walk or drive is so many minutes long and thus requires our departure be no later than a certain time in order to arrive on-time at our destination, which in turn gives us so much time to do this or that until the clock once more demands our departure. Ap-proaching deadlines and a dwindling number of hours with which to work demand that one's ra-tioned hours of sleep be temporarily cut-back, perhaps with the intention of "borrowing" hours from a later day such that the hours of sleep now sacrificed might be "made up" later. Un-planned events and possibilities that arise or oc-cur to us spontaneously show up as that for which we have no time, given that our day has already been allotted.

What then is lost when we treat a day as a mere 24 hours? On our walk or drive whose duration we've measured and memorized, the flora in bloom are banished to obscurity. Our many commitments and appointments which we have scheduled in advance and with which our days are filled rule out or even conceal altogether the fittingness of a particular day for foraging for wild mushrooms, or a particular evening for watching a thunderstorm from the porch. Due to prior scheduling, the solicitations of the first warm, sunny day after a long, harsh winter fall on deaf ears. The rationing of sleep and setting of alarms instrumentalizes sleep for productivity and so bears it as a (barely) necessary evil. To see sleep in such a way is to overlook other, much richer aspects of sleep: its bringing to a close one day and delivering us over to the next as fresh and distinct from the previous, with all of the potential and promise that brand new days bring; its restoration of our mind, body, and spirit that prepares us for the new day's summons; its offering of a glimpse into our deepest existential questions, concerns, and aspirations through the lens of dreams. The same can be said for the day itself: to see a day as a mere 24 hours is to overlook each day's richer dimensions and possibilities.

But what more is a day than 24 hours? It is said that the dawn of a new day is a fresh start—and indeed it is. But is this new start on a blank canvas? Not hardly.

Different days have different demands, different callings, and different affordances. The different demands, callings, and affordances that belong to each day are precisely what the 24-hour conception of a day overlooks. The first warm, sunny day after a long, harsh winter not only affords us the opportunity to return to out-door recreation, but indeed inspires and calls us to do so with an extraordinary insistence. The morning that is permeated with the sounds of heavy rain and thunder solicits us to spend a bit more time with our morning coffee and thoughts. The summer evening with a cool breeze, clear skies, and a scantly lit moon beck-ons us to go outside and look up toward the Heavens in awe—an ancient awe that is ever and always renewed. The day that follows a great tragedy or defeat affords us an occasion to reflect and the opportunity to re-collect and re-orient ourselves. The day after a great triumph or blessing affords us a most felicitous occasion in which to rejoice and to feel grateful.

It is abundantly clear that a day is most dearly embraced in terms of its particular character—a character seldom seen in advance and which is most difficult (indeed, more often than not impossible) to schedule in advance.

But schedule we must: deadlines loom, the kids' piano lessons are on set days of the week, and we are expected to be at work on time rain or shine, tragedy or triumph. Without scheduling, much of life would not be possible. But a schedule is not a gift to be cherished the way a day—and a lifetime—is. A gift is something to be cherished and not to be squandered. If on the first warm, sunny day of spring we get the call to go outside and play catch with a son who has patiently awaited this day all winter long—and we promptly hang up upon receiving that call—the gift of that day is lost. There may be more days to follow that will be suitable for playing catch, but few of them will have the ex-traordinary level of excitement that is intrinsic to the first break in the weather. Catch can be re-scheduled, but the excitement and relief of that first warm, sunny day cannot.

The more we default to what is sched-uled in advance, the more we will miss our daily miracles. The days—and the peculiar character that distinguishes each day—pass us by; over time, with the accumulated passing of many days on end, it is in turn *life* that passes us by. Moments are lost, memories are foreclosed upon and there is no making good on them.

And so what we schedule in advance must remain tentative as much as possible, lest we miss and so fail to live up to the gift that is each day, the gift that is a lifetime.

Learning

LEARNING AT GREAT DEPTH requires care and humility. Disinterest will quickly render one's learning stagnant, and absent the humility required to take seriously the idea that there is more for one to learn, any further learning will require a *humbling* of the would-be learner who lacked humility, a humbling in which they come face-to-face with what they have not yet mastered. The careless will stall-out and stagnate due to lack of interest, while the haughty and pretentious will inevitably be humbled in an alarming way and so find themselves faced with the choice of accepting the role of student once more—thus acknowledging that the peak they've reached was not the apex—or simply ceasing to learn.

But is it the apex we're after in learning? Perhaps, but are hiking and exploring in the mountains not enjoyable *even if* one does not

11

reach the summit specifically? Is hiking just about reaching the spot at the very top and looking down and out? Of course not; summiting the mountain is a goal we can have and a destination we can orient ourselves toward, but hiking is worthwhile outside of the destination. Do we *only* enjoy the moment we spend at the very top? Is the rest of the time spent just dutifully trudging along a trail to and from the summit?

Is learning to play an instrument about being the best in the world? Presumably not—if it were, a lot of musicians would despair, and playing music would not be the joyous form of recreation that it is for millions of people. Is learning an instrument even about *maximizing* your own potential to be the absolute best musician that *you* as an individual could possibly be? Presumably not—do we not learn an instrument and find immense joy in simply being able to play a tune and harmonize with others? Is the splendor and delight of making music really dampened by the fact that we could be better than we currently are? Does one learn carpentry with the sole intent to become a master carpenter? Or is it plenty satisfying and rewarding to build a humble home for oneself and to help friends in one's community do the same?

There is more to life than belongs to any particular domain. Even if you're the best violinist the world has ever seen, there is more to life than violin: Have you learned how to be a good friend? Have you learned to discern between good and bad, right and wrong? Have you learned how to deal with different types of people and navigate different sorts of situations? Have you learned how to deal with various tragedies and triumphs? Sometimes we need to hear music, and sometimes our neighbor needs our help with a construction project—and yet, our violin and construction skills are of little use when a friend comes to us in distress and seeking advice, or when we ourselves are trying to navigate a dilemma or determine a course of action.

There is quite a lot to learn—quite a lot that is *important* to learn. Indeed, our lives may well begin to look and feel impoverished—like something is missing—to varying degrees if we neglect to learn any number of important things. To live to learn is to seek this or that summit or several summits in succession; to *learn to live* is to learn so that we may live well —that we may be a hiking companion of the highest order, able to entertain and be entertained with good conversation, to offer assistance when needed or respond appropriately if a situation arises, and to duly appreciate the beauty and splendor behind every turn of the trail on the way to the summit.

Adventure

WHEN BILBO BAGGINS RETURNED from his adventure, the Shire no longer felt quite like home. Likewise, being a remarkably quaint and largely unadventurous—if a bit cheeky at times—place, the other Shirelings simply couldn't understand the Bilbo who had returned to them, so different from the one who'd departed so long ago.

As is apparent in the case of Bilbo Baggins, adventure changes those who pursue it. Indeed, this change, whatever it may be, seems to be the primary purpose behind adventure's pursuit—whether this is acknowledged ahead of time or recognized in retrospect. More than just travel to broaden our horizons, adventure's allure is the promise of perils and pitfalls, progress and purpose. When embarking on an adventure, there are infinite unknowns—and yet, somehow, there remain opaque guarantees of worthwhile trials, triumphs, and moments that will translate into treasured memories, tumultuous tales, and soul-building theodicies.

A theodicy is an understanding of *why* evil and tragedy exist in our world. Adventure is a profound, involved way of coming to such an understanding: the adventurer discovers firsthand that perils, evils, tragedies, and tribulations are occasions that afford us opportunities for profound growth. The trials of adventures test our souls: they test our courage, faith, willingness, and the strength of our commitment to remaining steadfast and true, to believe in what we're doing and to do what we believe in. Adventure's perils beckon our souls to rise to the occasion, to grow to meet the demands of the adventure. Adventure, as it were, is a way of *building* our souls up.

If adventure at its core amounts to a soul-building theodicy, we may think of adventure in its essence as a *theological odyssey*. Through the course of adventures, we become the person we are intended to become: by being beckoned to rise and meet many different challenges, our souls are called upon to grow in different ways; the adventure's demands dictate where we are to grow, and they instruct us with a sense of urgency. In its demands and dictates, adventure is a like forge and hammer; indeed, as adventures run their course it is common for someone to emerge unrecognizable from the day one embarked, having been repeatedly heated and wrought, worked into shape.

By the virtue of an adventurous spirit— by being eager to embark on an adventure and to time and time again double-down on the commitment to persevere through its perils—we discover and cultivate the person whom we are to become. Having been in and out of adventure's forge and having withstood being beaten into shape, Bilbo returned to the Shire nigh unrecognizable—and *this* is what made the many perils of his adventure worthwhile.

Work

WE HAVE TO WORK to earn our keep—earning a living is quite important. Indeed, it is also quite well-established that idle hands tend to find trouble, and so work also keeps us on the straight and narrow. Beyond the obvious lies an important question, however: is looking for work just about finding an occupation and getting paid? Is there perhaps some specific sort (or sorts) of work that we're *supposed* to do? If so, what is at stake in finding the work that we're *supposed* to do or *called to*? How do we even identify it?

The work one chooses to do matters. What if Aristotle decided not to pursue philosophical questions, instead focusing more on his work in medicine, biology, and literary criticism? Looking back at Thomas Jefferson's massive role in America's coming into its constitution as a new nation, is there not something *jar-*

ring about the idea that he could have chosen to be a full-time architect instead of a statesman? This isn't to suggest that medicine or architecture are lesser pursuits—rather the idea is that it borders on inconceivable for us to imagine that Aristotle or Jefferson might have chosen to focus on other work *in lieu of* their massively influential work that ultimately cemented their places in history.

Aristotle and Jefferson worked in these other fields, but these other fields were not, for either of them, what most would call their *life's work*. But there is a sense in which these works that occupied a lesser place in each of their lives may have very well prepared them for—or even been essential to—what we consider to have been their life's work. It isn't hard to imagine that Aristotle's work in medicine, biology, and literary criticism may well have granted him greater context and depth in his thinking about what is required for a human being to live well and flourish or his conception of the human soul —two of his most important philosophical undertakings. Nor is it difficult to imagine that Jefferson's work as a lawyer and architect prepared him for and helped shape his later work as a statesman, as an architect of a new nation and its legal system.

What ultimately turns out to be one's most important work—what we call one's *life's work*—is often prepared for and shaped by other work done along the way. Sometimes this preparation is part of our planning, but in many cases it is only later on in retrospect that we come to recognize the work that came before as having been necessary preparation for the work of today.

Even if it is not the work that ultimately defines our lives in retrospect, the work of today is in another sense one's most important work: it is *the work* we are to do *today*. It isn't the work of yesterday nor the work of tomorrow, it is the work we are presently confronted with and with which we are to engage in earnest. Even if it is the work of tomorrow that will define our lives, the work of today still has to be done. A life's work is not just a life's defining work, but also the rest of the work that prepared for it.

21

More important than simply finding work is finding the work of today. When we learn to find the work we are called to do *today* and we train ourselves to hear and answer *that* call, we are in another sense preparing, readying ourselves to hear our *calling* when it arrives.

Work II

HYPER-SPECIALIZATION OF THE WORKFORCE has rendered renaissance men exceedingly rare. The possibility that different types of work can prepare us for later work has been explored— but what about concurrent, complimentary works? People putting their nose to the ground and grinding away on a particular project and finding great success isn't at all uncommon— but is there some benefit to working on multiple, vastly different pursuits at once?

Consider intellectual pursuits, wherein there exists the danger of becoming divorced from the day-to-day, from life on the ground. The ivory tower's lofty offices are far from the dirt and rocks on which the tower stands and the view from up there is very different; might the intellectuals in its offices benefit from also working on the ground, digging into the dirt?

It's not their job in the sense that it's not what they're (at least primarily) paid to do—but might digging dirt make them better at *their* job? Presumably, intellectuals are paid for their intellectual pursuits because their pursuits are supposed to offer something to the rest of society. Inasmuch as ivory tower intellectuals are divorced from the day-to-day—the stomping grounds of most of society—it is not far-fetched to suppose that their works will be correspondingly less relevant to those on the ground. Indeed, the view from the tower is much different than the view from the ground; what appears relevant from one vantage point may not look like much—or even be visible at all—from another vantage point.

If they themselves do not have their feet planted firmly on the ground, how much do intellectuals really have in common with most of society? How could they expect to produce work of relevance and resonance to anyone outside of the other offices on their floor of the tower? Without boots on the ground, their capacity to relate to those whom they in part *owe* their intellectual contributions will be strained and diminished. Presumably the intellectuals did not themselves construct their towers and offices and, moreover, society's practice of specialized labor is only sustainable and harmonious when various specialized labors make contributions that are valued enough by other members of society to not draw popular indignation or indifference; specialized labors have to have value to people outside of the specialized field itself, and that value to others has to be appreciable. Among the things most conducive to ensuring (as best as one can) the relevance of intellectual pursuits to everyday life is for the intellectuals themselves to spend time living and working outside of their tower, on solid ground.

What does it mean to live and work on the ground? How might this supposed benefit to their various scholarly, legal, political, or otherwise intellectual pursuits be cashed out?

Living in the day-to-day is more than just paying bills and taxes and following along with this or that form of popular entertainment. Day-to-day *work* is the groundwork that societies are built on. The groundwork of societies includes: farming and other food-related work; carpentry, masonry, heating, plumbing, electrical work, and everything else that goes into building construction, maintenance, and repair; a variety of different types of trade-work and crafts; vehicle repair and maintenance; and other similarly necessary work for societies to be built and maintained, the vast majority of it being hands-on in nature.

How can these sorts of pursuits be of benefit to those who work primarily in offices, courtrooms, and diplomatic chambers? An economist who is also an avid woodworker will know that different types of woodworkers with different focuses each need to be able to acquire specific types of wood suited to their particular projects—not just any type of lumber will do. That same economist will also understand that while outsourcing the manufacturing of tools to cheaper labor markets may *seem* like a good idea in terms of production costs and quantities of tools produced, the consequences of flooding a market with cheap, mass-produced tools of poor quality will have a number of negative second and third-order effects on production, goods, and economies as a whole than someone who never works with tools could possibly imagine. A politician who also runs a farm will have a much better grasp of the needs of one of society's most important industries as well as the potential impacts of various legislative proposals on agricultural practices, traditions, productivity, and sustainability. This politician, together with the aforementioned economist, will be able to see and discern much more clearly between viable policies and public investments that make good use of in an area's natural resources and policies and public investments that disregard or even diminish the local resources. Their work on the ground thus informs their political and economic work, imbuing it with a first-hand grasp of what is important, what is possible, and what is likely to be prosperous or devastating for an area or an industry.

It may be suggested that *having lived* in the day-to-day in the past might be good enough; the farmer who becomes a scholar will have some understanding of what sort of intellectual contributions will be fruitful for farmers and philosophers alike. But resting on the laurels of past labor in hope that it will sustain indefinitely the relevance of one's intellectual endeavors is shaky ground: how easily time and distance can distort one's memories and impressions, putting one at risk of diminishing in retrospect the reality of work and toil, allowing one to remember fondly what was previously endured with much grinning and bearing. What is more, the well may run dry: while memories may offer us a great deal, continued engagement is perpetually fruitful in that it keeps open the possibility for new insight and is, of course, the best way to avoid forgetting (or seeing through rose-colored classes) what has already been learned firsthand.

But are there yet other reasons to engage with different types of work together, in a back-and-forth manner? Beyond the importance of keeping an intellectual grounded and in-touch with the day-to-day, digging dirt, shoveling shit, and fixing fences can redirect one's mind away from intellectual work and so serve as a reprieve in that regard, a pause that allows previous thoughts to simmer and settle and new thoughts time to make their way in. What is

28

more: when we exhaust ourselves both physically and mentally, we go to bed most *tired* and *happy*. Thinking and writing, digging and building are tiring and satisfying in very different ways, and to exhaust and enjoy ourselves in these different ways together will make us *most* tired and happy when the end of the day draws near. The more tired and happy we are when we lay our heads down, the more we are refreshed and made ready for the next day's work.

This all works both ways, of course: not only will the work of those in the tower be less relevant if they never dig into the dirt, but those with their feet firmly planted on the ground run the risk of banality if they never concern themselves with the arts, humanities, and other intellectual endeavors—that is, if they never let their minds wander about up in the clouds. Without making it a point to exercise the mind and give thought to things, without questioning, creating, and working to expand the horizons of our understanding of the world around us as well as our imaginations, we would be reducing ourselves to little more than less efficient automatons whose inability to match the sustained productivity of actual machines stems, in part, from the natural tendency of the mind to *want* to wonder and wander about.

The body and the mind both get stir-crazy if not exercised—it is best to give both their due, and beneficial in more ways than are immediately obvious.

Good Works

THAT THERE ARE GOOD WORKS lends itself to
the idea that there are also bad works—works
we may tentatively tie to the familiar phrase:
"ill-gotten gains." Easier to discern and to de-
scribe with a fair degree of precision, thinking
about the essence of *bad* works may lead us to a
more robust and fleshed-out conception of what
good works are.

　　When we think of ill-gotten gains, it
brings to mind profits that are attained dubi-
ously or at some disturbing expense to others.
"Disturbing" because if a carpenter builds a
quality deck for someone, it is naturally done so
at the client's expense—but not in any sense
that anyone is disturbed by. A loan-shark, however, who preys on someone already between a
rock and a hard place and—seeing opportunity
in the borrower's misfortune—demands a hefty
interest rate on the principal of the loan is prof-

iting at the expense of another in a way that is disturbing. Likewise, the carpenter who knowingly does sub-par work in the name of profit (via excessive mark-up on cheap materials, making future repair work more likely or necessary sooner, or simply rushing through jobs to squeeze more jobs in, etc.) is also profiting in a way that is distasteful. Worse yet are those who profit off the peddling of commodities of despair and yet even worse, among the most ghastly of all, are the many shanghaiers of human beings.

If bad works are disturbing and predatory, it seems that good works are honest and upbuilding. Just as a carpenter who does his best building a deck that will be host to barbecues and countless morning coffees and conversations, a friend or neighbor does his best to build up his friend or neighbor in a tough spot: this may mean giving guidance in a tumultuous time or helping to repair a damaged roof. While many of the good works we are capable of may involve little or no material gains, good works often lead to many other good things: doing good work is, first and foremost, both deeply satisfying and essential for human flourishing; it builds character. Doing good work with and for friends, neighbors, and loved ones often serves to strengthen our relationships and bonds with them and is among the very best ways to enrich our social lives and ties to our communities. These rewards and material gains are, of course, not at all mutually exclusive. As in the case of the good carpenter, good work is often paid well; a good carpenter will always have work to do from people willing to pay him well—but pay, when it is part of the reward for good work, is only ever *part* of the reward. Always present is the *upbuilding* satisfaction of having done *good*, having done something with the honest intention of a positive difference.

Beholding the fruits of our labor is a deeply satisfying part of good work's reward, and sometimes this is given to us immediately and other times by-and-by. Indeed, sometimes this comes in the form of simple, quiet knowledge that we planted a seed whose fruit we may never see, but will surely be *good* for those for whom it comes to fruition. The leaving of such a legacy, the gift of our labor in sowing seeds so that future generations may inherit fruit also gifts us something in return: the heartening comfort of greater hope, even perhaps a degree of assurance, that the future will be fruitful and good.

In their ill-gotten gains, doers of bad works have their reward in full.

A Home's Hearth

THE FOCAL POINT OF A ROOM MATTERS. As Albert Borgmann and others have pointed out, it is the focal point of a room—be it a dinner table, a hearth, or a television—that naturally orients the people in it, giving them directive as they enter: sit here, face that direction, tend to this or that, etc. In a dining room, the table will be the focal point that gathers and orients; the same can be said for a game room featuring a pool table. While common practice has maintained that a proper dining room is focused around a table, common practice regarding the family room or living room—perhaps the most important room in a home—has degenerated most grievously.

Most modern living rooms feature a television as the room's focal point. Such a living room will have a centrally located television with the furniture arranged around it such that, upon entering, the room's arrangement implicitly instructs individuals to orient themselves toward the TV. Before televisions, the focal point of family rooms tended to be a fireplace or a wood stove. When the hearth was the heart of a home, it focused the family living there in its own way, giving its own directive. It was first and foremost a place to gather in order to be warm during the winter months, but it also served as an important social setting: by the hearth books and letters were read aloud, stories were shared across generations, games and instruments were played, and important matters concerning the family were discussed. Tea and other beverages were prepared next to it, and the family's legacy, accomplishments, and keepsakes were displayed on the mantle above.

While the television draws the focus of those watching it *away* from the others next to them, the hearth is a focal point that shelters an *opening* before it. Unlike the TV, the hearth does not talk over us or demand our direct attention; rather, the hearth draws us into the warmth of its vicinity and turns our attention toward each other and various activities afforded to us by what is within reach: instruments, books, letters, games, tea, etc. The hearth provides a place for *engagement.* The hearth beckons us to be together in the heart of the home and it focuses family lifc around the various engagements its warm space fosters. It maintains a central, open space to engage with each other and all of the various engagements befitting a *living* room: music, company, books, games, etc. Just as the hearth is a *focal* point that focuses our presences and attention, Borgmann calls the various engagements it provides space for "focal practices"; these practices focus not just our attention, but our lives.

Television, on the other hand, is necessarily *disengaging.* At its best it can be interesting or exciting, but watching television is fundamentally passive: it is not actively *engaging* in the way conversation, instruments, games, or books are. Given that socializing and engagemcnt arc crucial for family life and living in general, television, with its anti-social and disengaging nature, is about the *last* thing we ought to organize our family rooms and living rooms around.

This isn't to say that a home's heart absolutely must be a hearth specifically, but whatever the heart of the home is, it should be a space that facilitates engagement with activities as well as each other.

Recreation

RECREATION IS A RE-CREATION of various pastimes, practices, arts, crafts, traditions, etc.

Though it is possible, this is not to suggest that we, in every instance, re-invent what it is that we are doing in ways that would somehow change what it means or entails to do whatever it is that we're doing. But at the very least, recreation is a re-creating in the sense of making manifest or bringing to fruition something that requires our playing a part to make it happen: we arrange a place to play a pick-up game and gather enough people and whatever equipment is needed and we play; we pick up our instruments and practice or play, perhaps calling other musicians to join in with us; we pick up and peruse an old book, re-discovering and re-imagining its contents as we read it once more.

Recreation infers a responsibility on our part to *make it happen*. Recreation requires our active engagement: we have to actively play or compete in this or that sport, practice this or that art, take up and become proficient in this or that instrument. This active engagement is what distinguishes recreation from entertainment. Entertainment is by-and-large passive; even with the possible exceptions of some specific movie or podcast that encourages us to think—and so engage in a thoughtful manner—the watching or listening is still primarily passive and, outside of perhaps certain vocabulary or other requisite knowledge, requires little to no preparation or skill; we press "play" and let it roll.

But if *mindless* entertainment—the most common form of entertainment, to be sure—fails to thoroughly engage and, indeed, rather *dulls* the mind, recreation makes use of and *sharpens* the mind. This sharpening is not only by virtue of recreation requiring our focus and mental engagement, but as we get more and more proficient in a particular domain, we are able not only to notice and re-create various patterns, but also to discover new patterns to put to use, new paths to pursue, and new possibilities to explore. These new patterns, paths, and possibilities that we discover make manifest a form of re-creating within the context of this or that recreational pastime or tradition.

Poverty

COVERED IN GREASE AND GRIME, I had little choice but to cancel classes one day due to some work I had begun on my car the day prior taking much longer than expected (as is, ironically, to be expected when working on cars); I simply would not have my car back together in time to go in to teach. The following class, one of my students asked me how it was that I'd learned to work on cars.

"Being poor," I replied. It was through being poor that I'd learned to do various forms of maintenance and repairs on vehicles. Indeed, just how much poverty actually affords us is quite surprising.

When the money in your wallet won't buy you much, the world beckons your ingenuity and willingness to get dirty and learn by doing—because what you're beckoned to do has to get done, and it won't get done if you don't do it. If it is hardly feasible to pay mechanics to do all of your car's maintenance and repairs, you've been afforded—in most compelling terms—the opportunity to learn how to work on cars. The less purchasing power at one's disposal, the more one is forced into learning, engagement, and resourcefulness. The more learned and resourceful one becomes through engagement across different domains, the more eager and confident one becomes in taking up new and different tasks.

The more one grows in competence and confidence across different domains, the better equipped one is to engage with one's community. When we've learned to work on cars, to take on basic construction and home maintenance projects, to farm, forage, or hunt our food, etc., we are in a position to provide such services and assistance to our neighbors, to engage with and serve our community closely and productively, working side-by-side with our neighbors and teaching them what we know and learning new things from them as well.

There are also other ways in which poverty pulls us into engagement with those in proximity: having less money for entertainment encourages us to seek recreation and rejoice in our own communities. Exotic vacations and expensive, big-name concert tickets may be cost-prohibitive, but potlucks and campfire tunes can be had at next to no cost. We may not have money to see the Rolling Stones, but for ten dollars we can go and see the talent that lives in our town, and we can have a drink with them after and enjoy friendly run-ins by-and-by—and we understand who they are, where they're from, and the meaning in their music much more intimately. On other occasions, we can see them around campfires and sing and play along.

Poverty's greatest asset is that compels us in the strongest terms to act on its many affordances. No amount of money can purchase initiative and, without initiative or impetus to learn and improve, a man is liable to become impotent—and indeed, poverty lends itself to fostering initiative quite well. If there is plenty of money for hiring out various work and taking destination vacations, we may never learn to do different types of rewarding work and we may travel the world over without ever getting to know our neighbors. If we can't afford to hire everything out or to travel the world over, we will walk out our door and down our street, we will run into neighbors, ask for and lend a helping hand, and find recreation in our communities, with those with whom our lives intertwine.

A Grounded Life

A STRONG FOUNDATION SITS ON SOLID GROUND. The deeper that something is dug into the ground or the more firm its footing—the more grounded something is—the more stable and durable it is. While no one would think to build a home without a foundation, far less often is thought given to the foundation of a *life*. What, then, is a *grounded life*? What does the foundation of such a life consist of?

Perhaps it will be easier to first imagine what a distinctly *un*grounded life might look like: not only would it surely have no roots, but it is easy to imagine it not even being *on* the ground—or at least not planted in it. It is imaginably a life filled with travel far and wide, perhaps by a person yet lacking in serious convictions or commitments and perhaps prone to be variously influenced or to go wherever the wind will take them. If such is a distinctly *un*-

grounded life, a grounded life will presumably be much the opposite: a life that is dug into and deeply rooted in a *particular patch of dirt*—a particular place that has a most privileged position in one's life: one's *home*. Presumably the grounded life is not only firmly entrenched in a particular place, but built upon a foundation of deep convictions, commitments, and forged bonds as well—it is not liable to be variously influenced, shaken, or blown about.

Once we find a place for ourselves and all the digging is done, the foundation of a life is constructed out of commitments. Out of commitments to our faith, our family, our work, our friends, our land, and our communities the foundation of a grounded life is built: we commit to putting faith into practice; we commit to growing, raising, providing for, and caring for our family; we commit to our work and to doing it well, because we do work we know to be important and that we believe in; we commit to being good friends and neighbors and good stewards of our land, both living off of it and preserving and cultivating its affordances as part of our legacy that we will leave for future generations; and finally, we commit to our communities in the forms of charity, service, and goodwill. Such a foundation is well-suited to endure and maintain its integrity through life's many, ever-changing seasons.

A life so grounded, with such a robust foundation, is as poised and unshakable as a life can be. But the stronger and deeper the foundation is, the less conducive it is to moving. A grounded life is *rooted*. From its roots and robust foundation a grounded life derives its strength, fortitude, and dignified disposition. If a grounded life is uprooted for transplant or some other reason, its roots will often require time to reestablish themselves, and some may die off altogether.

Dignified Indifference

INDIFFERENCE IS EASY ENOUGH TO GRASP, but what does it mean for indifference to be *dignified*? What does mere indifference look like, and how might dignity transform indifference?

To be dignified requires both having *and adhering to* a moral standard. Absent a standard of behavior that one adheres to, dignity would have no basis; there would be nothing in which any dignity could be sufficiently grounded, nothing to qualify any dignity beyond what is called "basic human dignity." Likewise, because there would be no behavioral ground for dignity without some standard of behavior, there would also be no behavior that would *deprive* one of dignity; in other words, everyone would have only "basic human dignity"—nothing more and nothing less, with no variation from person to person.

For example, it is believing in and culti-vating the virtue of temperance that makes an individual who drinks socially and responsibly dignified in comparison to the individual who drinks until he falls off his bar stool. Not adher-ing to a respectable moral standard regarding alcohol and moderation is what makes the drunkard comparatively undignified, and reme-dying such behavior would in turn *restore* his dignity. In the meantime, while the drunk may have the same basic human dignity as everyone else, his present behavior could hardly be called dignified.

Indifference alone is merely a lack of concern for the ways, dealings, attitudes, and expectations of others. *Dignified* indifference is a lack of concern for the ways, dealings, atti-tudes, and expectations of others while simulta-neously having and holding oneself to a more worthy standard of behavior. Without dignity to back up indifference, indifferent individuals are liable to drown in debauchery. For a vivid ex-ample, let us consider the counter-culture movement of the 1960s and '70s: their biggest problem wasn't that they were wrong about the war (indeed, they weren't at all wrong on that account) or burning their draft cards. Rather, their biggest problem was that they were terrible messengers despite having a very important message to deliver. As a consequence of many of their behaviors—which betrayed a lack of any widely respectable moral standard—much of society did not take them seriously; much of society did not *respect* them enough to take them seriously and consider their message. Without adhering to a respectable moral standard—without dignity—they drowned in the depths of debauchery, dragging their message down with them.

But what if the hippies who protested the Vietnam war had been dignified? What if it was hundreds of thousands of commonly respectable, dignified individuals who burned their draft cards and refused to partake in a most questionable war? If such was in fact the case, if the message had been delivered by more dignified messengers, it would be a very reasonable wager to suppose that a much greater number of people would have embraced the anti-war message. Alas, what was widely received of the counter-culture's message amounted to a mere indifference to society's longstanding norms—cultural, moral, and otherwise—without any decisive or commonly desirable direction accompanying it.

Dignified indifference, on the other hand, has a positive direction: it is not just a rejection of what others are up to, but a rejection *in favor of* something higher or more noble. It is indifference for the ways, dealings, attitudes, and expectations of others *in favor of a different way of going about life* that has, as its basis for dignity, a higher moral standard than that of those whom one is indifferent toward. It is not the sort of directionless indifference described above, but a *directed* indifference: one is indifferent toward what others are doing and the expectations others have of one to follow suit *because* one has a better direction and is walking a better path. In other words, having a higher moral standard gives one a better direction for one's life and the path others are walking is recognized as comparatively less dignified. What others are up to and expect one to join in on is irrelevant because one has found a better direction to go in, a better path to follow.

Dignity thus gives indifference a positive direction while indifference alone, or *un*dignified indifference, is more or less wayward, a mere rejection without direction—or at least any positive direction. Dignity thus transforms indifference into a rejection-turned-upbuilding; in dignified indifference one *assumes responsibility* for his or her indifference and thus takes on the work of *upbuilding*: building up one's character so to rise to meet—and then maintain —a higher standard of behavior that dignity demands of an individual.

Magnificence

A NECESSARY VIRTUE for living well and flourishing, Aristotle describes magnificence as a sort of large scale generosity or being generous in a big way to one's community, city, nation, etc. The magnificent individual is one who gifts his community something great, something of sizable benefit to the public good. One of the examples Aristotle gives is covering the costs of constructing and commissioning a warship for the nation's navy (the city's navy in his day, but you get the idea).

Needless to say, there are not very many individuals who can afford to buy their nation a battleship or an aircraft carrier—but is such an example really a viable or even sensible standard for assessing whether or not someone benefits his community in a magnificent manner? What can we do for our communities that is greatly generous, but not unfathomably beyond our financial means?

Aristotle's example of donating a warship is not just about its great cost, but also its great contribution to the city's common good—in this case by bolstering the city's defenses (and for Athens in particular, the city's famously formidable navy was the cornerstone of her defenses). If we want to avoid tying magnificence to millions of dollars, we can instead think of magnificence as—more fundamentally—a great contribution to our community's common good. The next question to consider is: what contributions of this sort, then, are within every man's reach?

In a tiny river town, a few people donating their time, resources, and know-how to build a well-constructed public pavilion or boat launch will give the community a little more life in a lasting way. A pavilion will provide families and the broader public with a place for gatherings and celebrations, while engagement with the river town's defining feature—the river—will be encouraged and facilitated by the construction of a boat launch. Anybody—just about anywhere—with a small patch of dirt can establish a community garden and invite people from their community to come and learn to grow food as well as share in and bond over timeless work and, as a result, eat well for little or no cost. A few musicians can donate their time and talents—and, in a sense, all the time it took to develop those talents—to entertain the community free of charge on this or that occasion. A couple who are well-versed in dancing can spend two hours a week teaching their neighbors to move with grace and elation under the local pavilion.

All of the aforementioned breathe new, lasting life into a community: magnificent contributions indeed.

A Year

YEARS HAVE THEIR OWN NARRATIVES that take
shape, with their own chapter markers along the
way. Be they seasons or semesters, the chapters
of a year are natural opportunities for our respective plots to transition to a new scene or
even take on an altogether different trajectory.
All said and done, a year in the books has
bound together its chapters in a continuity: this
chapter and its context and challenges leading
into the next chapter, with its own context and
challenges, work to be done, lessons to be
learned, and memories to be made. Just as these
chapters often refer back to prior chapters, a
year in the books will often reference prior
books in the series; in retrospect we can see
most clearly how prior chapters and books indeed foreshadowed the chapters and books that
follow.

The unfolding of a year's story—with its pace, its extension across time, and its coherent continuity—affords us sufficient time to develop both ourselves and our part in the plot. Just as a ship cannot turn on a dime unless it is tossed and whipped around by winds and waves in the midst of a storm, it is rare for an individual to make a sharp turn in his trajectory in a single day without some outside intervention. Across a year, however, an individual can adjust course and take on a different trajectory. A year is time enough to live and learn, and time enough to be tested over a considerable span of time. Though a lesson may be in some sense learned in a single day, a lesson's *staying power*—its being learned and ingrained such that it *lasts* and is *brought to bear on our lives*—is only evident over the course of time.

If such staying power is to be had, a sort of *resoluteness* will be required of us. This is why a new year's *resolution* is much less a decision about something and much more a commitment to some lesson learned that we wish to see through, that is, bring to bear on our lives.

A new year's resolution demands of us resoluteness.

Without resoluteness to back up a resolution, the book that is a year will be less likely to advance the plot of our lives in a significant way. Indeed, it is likely in such cases that the book in question and its chapters will resemble all too closely those that came before it.

Fear and Faith

FEAR AND FAITH ARE FURTHEST APART, yet the space between them is among the fastest-traveled distances we know. In an instant it is possible to go from one to the other and back again. How might it be that we can go back and forth between them so?

Though fear creeps into the present, it is largely concerned with the future: that which is not yet, and which is not yet known definitively. Typically, fear concerns particular possibilities, often regardless of their actual likelihood. But fear also concerns the unknown and the unknowable as such, as well as the perceived possibility of the total absence of possibilities—or at least "viable possibilities"—altogether. When we are fearful about the future, we are prone to hesitancy, uneasiness, and even paralysis—being "paralyzed by fear." Even after acting, fear will have us questioning whether or not we made the right decision; will things indeed end as we intended, or at least favorably? Will we indeed avoid the thing we feared via the choice we made in its shadow?

Faith, too, though felt with all of its comfort in the present, is primarily concerned with the future. Faith, however, seems to require a recognition of the future *as such*: as *not yet* and yet uncertain. As opposed to fear of the unknown, with its characteristic hesitancy and uneasiness, faith concerning the unknown is accompanied by anticipation, readiness, and excitement. Still without foresight, faith is open to the unknown, all the while privy to the knowledge that things often work out better than one could have imagined in advance. Faith is faith that *despite not knowing* exactly how things will turn out or how things will take shape, that things will ultimately end well; but this faith that things *will* end well seems to carry with it the requirement that we *act in faith*. Faith compels us to act entirely differently from the ways in which fear encourages us to act; indeed, fear and faith both, by their respective natures, discourage and disparage the actions belonging to the other.

Fear entices a person to shy away from this or that possibility because of the worry that things may ultimatcly cnd badly, or because it is hard to imagine, in the present, the positive turns that things might take following the coming to fruition of whatever possibility one is afraid of. On the contrary, if fear has us avoiding, faith has us steadfastly advancing: faith beckons us forward with the acknowledgment that we cannot foresee how the future will unfold and the assurance that we *do not know* that things will end badly—and, indeed, things could very well turn out *better* than we could have imagined, in ways we could not have foreseen. While fear in the face of an undetermined future focuses on the possibility of things turning out badly, faith is keenly aware of the inherent promise that thc futurc always holds: the future always has potential for wonderful outcomes that are, in the present, necessarily unforeseeable—we simply cannot imagine all the good things that could—and, indeed, often do—happen. In faith there is the knowledge that the future has not only the possibility of peril, but also the promise of hidden potential that is just as inherent. Faith's acknowledgment and embrace of the future's inherent promise, of its unforeseen potential, empowers us to choose and act on a basis other than avoidance of this or that feared outcome.

With the unknown future not being the deterrent that it is in fear, faith frees us to choose not in relation to this or that possible outcome, but instead out of deeper convictions concerning what it is we feel—or on some level know—that we must do, independent of concerns about how things might work out. When we choose and act from a position of faith, we are freed from concerns of the future and delivered over to conviction: we choose not based on an imagined future, but on the basis of what our convictions call us to do in the present, independent of imagined outcomes. Freed to act out of our convictions, faith compels us forward with courage, resolve, and excited curiosity about what the future may hold. Freed from fears about the future, we act faithfully in the present

—where faith comforts and compels us to go forward with courage and resoluteness.

Despite enabling us to choose and act on a basis other than the future, in being faithful there is most of all *hope* for the future. All the more so is there hope because faith and conviction sure up our footing and steady our hands in action—sure footing and steady hands, it turns out, are much more suitable for action and success than the unsure footing and shaky hands; indeed, someone shaking in their boots is hardly able to advance, let alone triumph. Rather, when we act in good faith and have its sure footing we are in the best position possible from which to press forward. In faith and its freeing us to act on our convictions with sure footing and calm, ready hands, we choose and act and advance from a position of power. A boxer who resolutely advances with courage, consistency, and tenacity and who maintains a strong base from which to repeatedly attack has infinitely more hope against a formidable opponent than any boxer who steps into the ring with unsure footing.

But how is it that a fearful coward may become faithfully empowered? As was said, though fear and faith are furthest apart, the distance between them is among the fastest-traveled distances we know. In both fear and faith, we are most familiar with the feeling commonly described as "butterflies." In both fear and faith, butterflies begin their fluttering in the pit of our stomachs; the question is where the butterflies go from there. In fear, the butterflies are confined inside and flutter incessantly and impatiently, the reverberations of their wings rendering us shaky inside and out; in faith we allow the butterflies to fly up and out and lead the way forward.

Prayer

IN PRAYER, we hold our hopes and aspirations up to God. When we do so at our best, we are not merely holding them up as if we were holding a genie in a bottle and making a wish; rather, we at the first instance hold our hopes and aspirations up to God so that they may be measured and weighed for us.

Is the hope or aspiration that I'm holding up to God worthy? Does it concern something trivial, a matter of little consequence? Is what I hope for or aspire to *good*? Am I asking God for something that is in alignment with His will? Is *my will* in alignment with His?

In the first moment of prayer, if we are listening, there is a sense of the answer to these questions and others. If we are willing to listen and open to what comes to us in that moment, it can at times be found that holding our hopes and aspirations up to God to be measured by

Him—rather than hastily asking away—is a gesture that can serve as a way of asking God to guide us.

If it is understood in that moment that what was held up is out of alignment or otherwise amiss, then we are in the same instance led closer to what *is* in alignment with His will—and so we are led closer to what God wills for us by virtue of humble hesitation—rather than hubris and haste—in beginning our prayer. In this way, prayer is understood as a standing under God, holding up what is hoped for with the more immediate intention of listening for His guidance and humbly, faithfully allowing our hopes and aspirations to be properly aligned.

With this intention, there are times when immediate clarity comes over us and also times when a certain ambiguity or mystery remains. For example, it may be clear enough that this or that hope held up to Him is *good* and well-intentioned, yet the question of whether it is what He intends to hand down to us may well remain; such is the mystery of what He has in store for us.

PRAYER

In the face of this mystery, we arrive at a most faithful prayer: a prayer for whatever it is that God intends for us.

Possible and Impossible Possibilities

ARE ALL POSSIBILITIES TRULY POSSIBLE? If
not, what is it that makes a possibility *genuinely*
possible? Surely there is a statistical possibility
of various random events occurring, but the
question of whether or not this or that possibility is genuinely possible pertains specifically to
existential possibilities: possibilities for who and
what we can become, what we can do with our
lives.

It is technically possible for anyone to
become an author, but even so becoming an author is only *really* possible if you first learn to
read and write and become articulate enough to
effectively communicate ideas—and then, of
course, those ideas have to be put into a book
or some other piece of publishable writing. If
you don't have something to publish, the "possibility" of being an author is not yet actually
possible; until one is actually writing something

and preparing it to be read by others, one simply won't be an author no matter how much
time goes by. It simply will not happen—without writing, the possibility of being an author is,
in a very real sense, impossible; it is an *impossible possibility*.

Heidegger tells us this about the nature
of possibilities in *Being and Time*: existential
possibilities only become truly possible upon
our projecting ourselves onto them—or *living
into them*. Heidegger refers to this self-projec-
tion (or what we might call "diving in") as *understanding*—for Heidegger, "understanding" is
what first cements a possibility as *actually possible for us*. One will never become an author if
one does not write, nor will one ever become a
musician without taking up an instrument. Heidegger's insight here seems undeniable: existential possibilities require a commitment on our
part in the form of *living into them* before they
have any possibility of becoming actual—before they become properly *possible*.

Clearly, it is important to live into hith-
erto impossible possibilities in order to render
them truly possible, but is it also important to

preserve other impossible possibilities *as* impossible? Of course we simply do not have the time to pursue every possibility, but beyond that, if we fail to understand the importance of *preserving the impossibility* of various possibilities—if we allow ourselves to *entertain too many possibilities*—we are liable to become dispersed in the dizzying dilemma of endless possibilities.

Is it a possibility for me to become a physician if I upend and reorient my life in that direction? Sure. The more relevant question is: is it a possibility worth my living into and making possible? Being able to live into only a relative handful of the infinite number of yet impossible possibilities, the overwhelming majority of these impossible possibilities must remain so; unless there is a most compelling reason for one impossible possibility to warrant our pursuit—thereby making it a *possible* possibility— why not expend that effort and focus onto an impossible possibility that *is* most compelling? We have to discern which impossible possibilities really matter, really compel us, and are worthwhile to pursue—and differentiate these from the impossible possibilities that are simply *not for us*, not fitting with the overarching order, integrity, and context of our lives.

Though we must first have the courage to pursue impossible possibilities before they will become possible, we also have to curb our curiosity and be willing to let most impossible possibilities fall away altogether in order to focus our efforts. Indeed, failing to do so can also distract us from *already possible* possibilities; it is possible—even common—to get so dizzy and caught up in a sea of impossible possibilities that one overlooks already possible possibilities —the ones already lived into to some degree or other. Indeed, it is often the case that the possibilities we've already lived into are among the most viable and choiceworthy possibilities before us.

By the time we're of the age where existential possibilities are of concern, it is more than likely we've already got at least a few possible possibilities under our belts: instruments we've learned, activities we've enjoyed, work we've assisted with, etc. These possibilities least of all should be overlooked. They are, after all, already part of *who we are*. If instead of diving into one of these already possible possibilities —or pursuing a particular, most compelling impossible possibility—we opt to instead dive into a *sea* of impossible possibilities, there is great risk of drowning—but also the potential for discovery of things not yet even hinted at.

Not everyone who dives into a sea of impossible possibilities will drown, but it is a sink-or-swim situation—and the longer one is in the sea, the more likely the possibility of sinking.

Salvaging Squandered Blessings

WHAT IS IT TO SQUANDER A BLESSING? When we recognize that we've been graced with a blessing, accompanying our gratitude is a responsibility to live into or make good on our blessings. There is a sense in which our gratitude requires us to be accountable for our blessings—to not reject them, to not take them for granted, to not let them go to waste—to not squander them.

To squander a blessing is to fail to hold up our end of the bargain concerning the blessing bestowed. Blessings, like being born into life itself, are a form of agreement made *for us* on our behalf, yet which we are no less party to or responsible for. To say that we are responsible for something is not limited to the sense of having directly caused or played a part in something's coming about; as Sartre pointed out, for the people of France World War II was *their* war and *they were responsible for it*. That is, they were responsible for what they made of it. Their lives were not postponed or on sabbatical until the war was over—they all had to live and make choices in regard to and in the context of the war. These choices would ultimately shape, in part, the significance of the war in each of their lives. They did not have to cause or agree to the war in order to be responsible for the choices they made in light of it.

Likewise, we do not have to ask for a blessing in order to be responsible for it. If we fail to make good on our end of the deal—if we squander our blessing—how might we then salvage a blessing once it is squandered?

Sometimes there's the hope that if we make good on our end of the deal *now*, the blessing that was squandered may yet be salvaged more or less as it was given. Other times, it's clear that the ship has sailed—or more precisely, been scuttled and subsequently entombed on the ocean floor. In such cases, the salvaging then is generally not an attempt to raise the ship, but something more akin to receiving a message-in-a-bottle that escaped entombment.

82

The ship may be gone, but we still get the message; the question, then, is what we do with it. Indeed, the message is most often a reaffirming of the responsibility we had to hold up our end of the bargain in the first place. It is made apparent that just because we let the ship we were sent sink, it doesn't mean we're free from the obligations that would have kept it afloat in the first place.

If there is any hope at all of raising a ship, it is through receiving and adhering to its final message, its reiteration of our original obligations. Even so, it is exceedingly rare and most miraculous for a ship itself to be salvaged once it has sunk. If, for example, an incredible work opportunity comes one's way and is squandered as a result of not putting forth the effort required to meet the new opportunity's demands, it is unlikely that the opportunity will be able to be later recovered—far more ships remain on the ocean floor than are successfully salvaged. Miracles do happen, however, and sometimes outside help arrives unexpectedly and most graciously and so a sunken ship, a squandered blessing, may be raised where one person alone could not. It is imperative in such instances, however, to make ready to not make the same mistakes twice, to not lose a second time what was lost and then found again in a miracle.

Even if a squandered blessing is never wholly salvaged as it was first given, owning up to the message reminding us of our obligations that we failed to meet—and now rising to meet them in the blessing's absence—we salvage much of what was meant for us in the first place: the obligations, which, in good time, bear their own fruit if we own up to them. In doing so, we thereby ready ourselves for the arrival of the next ship and orient ourselves with a watchful eye toward the horizon. Indeed, there is now room for another ship to come into port, and we need to be ready for its arrival.

Shame

SHAME CAN HELP US FIND OUR BEARINGS. Feeling ashamed is something we generally try to avoid by steering clear of shameful actions in the first place. For some, another way of attempting to avoid shame is what might be called living "shamelessly": committing shameful actions, but with accompanying denial or rejection of any shame. But such "shameless" living will ultimately only amount to self-degradation and the lack of any basis for self-respect or dignity. The good news is that dark cloud of shame has a silver lining—but this silver lining requires us to see shame through rather than shrug it off, reject it, or run from it. If we flee from shame as if it were a bogeyman, it will never help us find our bearings.

The "relief" from "shrugging off" shame would be akin to the "relief" from fleeing anxiety. It is not any sort of genuine relief, but a perpetual struggle to ignore that which is pro-foundly disquieting. Genuine relief, on the other hand, requires one to answer shame's solicita-tions rather than trying to ignore them. What are shame's solicitations, and what does answer-ing them entail?

Shame solicits individuals to take a stance on themselves, and answering its solicita-tions entails precisely that. In many cases, shame is experienced as soliciting individuals to take a *particular* stance on themselves—and that stance is plainly obvious. If a soccer coach sees that one of his most talented players is coasting on talent alone, not putting in much effort, and so shames the player for it, the shame the player feels (assuming he feels ashamed) solicits him to take a stance on him-self, indeed a *particular* stance: that of being a talented athlete who, currently skating by on tal-ent, needs to put in the necessary work in order to make the most of his gift and not let his coach, his teammates, as well as himself down. Indeed, the fact that others have noticed and effectively shamed him lets him *know* that the possibility of him letting everyone down is both real and foreseeable—and he is responsible for this possibility and its prevention.

That *this particular stance* is the one that shame solicits the individual to take on himself and that it is *immediately obvious* is common in many instances of shame. *Committing* to that stance which shame solicits the player to take up and so *seeing the shame through* is the positive turn and road to relief. The soccer player feels shame and is solicited by it to take a particular stance on himself that, in his committing to it, allows him to see the shame through *so to emerge as an individual for whom that shame is no longer applicable in the present* (i.e., the player commits himself to the perspective shame led him to and so becomes hardworking, which in turn will bring him to a point where the shame he felt is no longer warranted).

But things are not always so clear and obvious as in the case above. Consider a student who is being shamed by his parents for getting a poor grade in calculus, a class that he is not particularly fond of. At first he feels ashamed at having let his parents down and performing poorly by conventional standards, but perhaps it isn't clear to him that he ought to buckle down and get to work the way such a stance was the clear solicitation for the soccer player. That might appear as a *possible* stance, but not the obvious one that ought to be taken. The feeling of shame is all the while rather unpleasant, and in order to find relief a stance must be taken. It's already clear to the student that calculus is not much fun and as it stands he's not very good at it—but that's not all there is to him. Let's assume he's got other worthwhile things going for him: perhaps he's doing great in other classes and has been accepted to the school and program of his choice, or maybe he's already taken quite a serious interest in woodworking and has lined up an apprenticeship at the carpenter's guild. In thinking about his poor grade not as an isolated matter, but instead in the greater context of his life and alongside other relevant considerations, he ends up adopting a stance on himself that amounts to him being a competent individual with things going for him—things that he cares about, is dedicated to, and works hard at—who happens to be doing poorly in a particular class that, in the big picture, is *largely* irrelevant.

All things considered, his receiving a bad grade in calculus is greatly outweighed by many positive things and, in the greater context of his life, is really not that important and cer-tainly not anything warranting the *continued* weight of shame. This does not mean it is okay to give up on secondary classes and endeavors altogether—indeed the initial experience of shame confirms that his receiving a poor grade in calculus was *not good* and *not desirable.* His navigation of the shame, however situated the incident and his accompanying shame within the greater context of his life. It is not good to earn a "D" in calculus, but it is also not the end of the world for an aspiring carpenter. Showing up to work hungover and injuring yourself, however, would warrant a much more signifi-cant amount of shame and for a greater dura-tion. Its navigation would require adopting a stance on oneself and solidifying that stance: e.g., becoming more disciplined, getting one's drinking in check, and maintaining a higher em-phasis on safety while working.

But is this not all simply "shrugging it off"? No. But what is the difference, then? The difference is that the student was not merely averse to shame—he acknowledged something negative, felt ashamed, and took the time to navigate his shame and thus took up a stance on himself. He *saw it through*. He didn't try to "shrug it off" in some maneuver of practiced nonchalance, nor did he try to simply ignore the feeling or muster up great indignation toward those shaming him as if the shaming itself constituted some a moral wrong. He took the time to experience it, think about it, and take up a stance on himself. The shaming afforded the individual in question an opportunity to grow as an individual. To navigate shame is necessarily to acknowledge it—not to deny it or any associated wrongdoing. Indeed, properly navigating shame requires to address in some way whatever wrongdoing was associated with the shame experienced and thus orient ourselves and move forward accordingly—whether this be as easy of a task as that of the calculus student, or as serious and sustained as that of the injured carpenter.

Shame, an unpleasant thing, can be, at least in most cases, *owned up to* and *seen through* such that one thereby arrives at and commits to a stance on themselves that is oriented toward genuine relief from shame. This process not only allows for the passing of the unpleasantness of shame, but also enables individuals to learn about and better themselves as well—to make good on or to correct going forward the mistakes of the past. But in order to see shame through and emerge knowing oneself better in light of it, one must not shy away from it by attempting to flee or write it off; it is necessary to recognize its importance and receive it as an opportunity to re-orient ourselves.

Passion

PASSION IS DISCOVERED in a spark, and after its ignition it sustains us in this or that pursuit, this or that place, or with this or that person. Through ups and downs, passion pulls us along; it carries us to new peaks and guides us through the valleys between, reminding us that even in a valley, we're still in the mountains, at high elevation.

Indeed, passion can even render the ups and downs superfluous to a degree: when we're passionate about something, the passion keeps us engaged come what may—the outcomes can appear neither here nor there; we are simply compelled and captivated. Winning can become something extra, an added adornment; losing par for the course, of little deterrence. Indeed, passion is often encountered as purpose enough to put one foot in front of the other, onward.

Passion is also precarious, however, and its perils and pitfalls are difficult to see at passion's speed. It can carry us up and away—from other things that matter to us, even things that we care about very deeply. On some occasions, this actually ends well and we are carried away to genuinely greener pastures—but more often when passion carries us away, we lose—and lose big—in a way that *matters*, that is significant and jarring enough to give our passion pause. This is a frequent occurrence with competing passions, such as when a pursuit beckons us away from a person or place and vice versa. It happens that sometimes we get so carried away by a passion, that other important parts of our lives become neglected and sometimes even lost altogether. Sometimes we have to choose, and sometimes a choice is seemingly made for us; indeed, passions sometimes run their course after carrying us so far, at which point there is often another passion that appears like a connecting flight to take us further along our way, in a different direction.

But the question remains: how might we reign passions in? Would that defeat their purpose? How might we avoid passion's perils and pitfalls? Ought we reject some passions altogether? How can we distinguish between good passions and bad passions?

To avoid passion's perils and pitfalls, our passions have to be integrated into a grounded and well-rounded life. Indeed, such is the natural course of life: over time, as we discover and pursue and cultivate many different passions, we can recognize in retrospect that as captivating as this or that passion was at the time, there were ultimately other, greater passions alongside or beyond it: passions that mattered more, were weightier and more worthwhile, and which fit much better into the context of a grounded, well-rounded life. In some such instances, it is apparent that a certain passion was of great danger or detriment to the sort of life that is grounded and flourishing—from such reflections on dodged bullets and difficult lessons, we learn the importance of discerning the promising passions from the precarious ones.

In instances where it is apparent that this or that passion, while good and fun and worthwhile, has run its course and fallen away in favor of yet more worthwhile passions, it becomes apparent that there are always more—and sometimes even more worthwhile—things for us to become passionate about. When we realize that life's affordances and its yet-to-be-discovered passions are inexhaustible, we thus become passionate about *life itself*. We become captivated *by life* and its myriad offerings, and the great richness and depth of certain offerings in particular. The question is no longer one of competing, specific passions, but that of a *passionate life*.

In the context of a *life* that is lived passionately, various formerly competing passions forfeit their pretensions—and, in some cases, forfeit their positions and give way altogether—and harmonize within the context of and for the sake of a grand composition in which they each occupy a dignified, yet unassuming place. Such a grand composition is a life well-lived.

Authenticity

THERE IS A JEWISH PARABLE about a rabbi named Zusya:

> Lying on his deathbed, Zusya was despondent and deeply distraught. His pupils, perplexed, asked him, "Zusya, what is the matter? You were almost as faithful as Abraham and almost as wise as Moses -- surely you will be judged favorably!"

> Zusya responded to his pupils: "I do not fear that God will ask me, 'Why weren't you more like Abraham?' or 'Why weren't you more like Moses?' I fear that God will ask me, 'Why weren't you more like Zusya?'"

This parable raises the concern that beyond a moral standard that we are to live up to, there is also a question of whether or not we meet a standard that is unique to each of us: did we, in fact, become who we are? Did we ultimately amount to what we, as particular individuals, were intended and had most peculiar potential to be?

Certainly we should all strive to cultivate various virtues such as faith, wisdom, courage, temperance, generosity, etc. We all have the potential to cultivate these and other virtues, and indeed an obligation to. But if we also have different potential and obligations concerning who we are to be and what we are to do with our lives as individuals, then in addition to being moral, we have an existential obligation to be authentic, to be who we are as *individuals*.

So what is it then to be authentic, to be an individual? Is it just speaking our minds? Is the person who dreamed of being an artist but succumbed to a career in accounting living authentically just by virtue of speaking freely and frankly? Presumably not. There is a sense in which someone with great potential and passion for something is living a lie—or under an "assumed identity" of sorts—if they forgo that pursuit, opting instead for something that does not align with their particular talents, potential, and passions.

To overlook or forego talents, potential, and passions seems a surefire way of precluding oneself from becoming who one is (or who one is *supposed* to be). Indeed, all three of these things seem to be *givens*—that is, we do not *choose* talents, potential, or passions for ourselves. Rather, these things are *discovered.* To say that talents, potential, and passions are discovered implies that they existed somewhere in or about us *all along*—that they are inherent, lying inchoate, waiting to be discovered and cultivated. This is to say that when we discover talents, potential, and passions, it is not a matter— or even a possibility—of choosing to have this or that talent or to be passionate about this or that thing. One does not elect to have immense talent in drawing or math or wrestling, rather talent's presence or absence is simply apparent given the right circumstances. One does not *decide* that the banjo is the instrument for them— oh, Heavens, no! Those individuals find themselves with an innate passion for the instrument. The individual innately drawn to the banjo cannot simply *decide* to be drawn to guitar instead, if he was not already innately drawn to it as well. Our *innate* talents, passions, and potential are discovered as *given* or made available to us —not as characteristics we chose to have.

He who has a passion for art, along with talent and potential, and who nonetheless abandons himself to accounting is surely not authentic—he is turning *away* from parts of who he is that were given to him. Now ultimately we will all have to forego certain passions and talents in pursuit of other passions and talents—that's just part of life's finitude. While foregoing certain passions and talents in pursuit of some other, more compelling passion or talent is hardly inauthentic, *abandoning oneself* to a pursuit for which one has no passion (and perhaps no exceptional talent, either) is most certainly an inauthentic rejection of given, important, individuating aspects of one's identity: one's peculiar gifts.

So what is each of us supposed to do? It's less a matter of figuring and more a matter of *finding* and *acknowledging*. What were we gifted with? Are there things we are naturally inclined to do that others really appreciate? Are there things we can we do that most others cannot? What work or engagements bring us joy? What makes sense to us that others do not see, but ought to?

When talking of gifts and blessings, it is often said that "my cup runneth over"—perhaps the fullest meaning of this phrase is that the gifts we've been given fill up our cups, then *runneth over onto the world*. That is to say, when we really live into the gifts we've been given our cup no longer contains them—they're not just in *our cup* anymore—and they run out onto the world, becoming not just gifts for us as individuals, but gifts given to the others *through* us.

To be who we are intended to be is to embrace and cultivate the many gifts that individuate us and thereby live into the potential that they afford us—that is, to become the individual that each of us has most peculiar potential to be, to *become who we are*. If we fail to become who we are—if we fail to be authentic in this way—we fail not only ourselves, but others. Our gifts are to be shared, indeed they are in a sense gifts that we are *entrusted* with and intended to bring to fruition and share with oth-

101

ers. In this way, the purpose that we serve—the gifts we cultivate and share with others and the ensuing effects—is intertwined with the passions, talents, and other gifts we've been given.

When we embrace the gifts with which we were entrusted and they spill out onto the world, truly then has one's cup runneth over.

Ersatz

THE WORD "SUBSTITUTE" IS OFTEN PRECEDED BY "CHEAP" for good reason. Though restaurants and other businesses have cheerfully marketed the idea of substitutions and endless options to consumers under the assumption that the mere existence of more and more choices is somehow inherently good, the fact remains that any and every substitute only *is* in relation to the real thing that the substitute stands in for. Every substitute is a stand-in for something real, something actual, or something original.

That substitutes are stand-ins by nature positions them by default as a second or third option. Marketing campaigns do their best to portray substitutes as, "even better than the real thing!" and while such a claim may generate sales, the truth of the matter is more or less always the opposite. Consider just about any example of things for which substitutes have been found:

Fast food and microwaves have been marketed as cheap, time-saving alternatives to meals prepared at home or by a chef at a sit-down restaurant. Endless entertainment from television, computers, and other devices has been made readily available as a stand-in for recreation—of course, without the need for the skills that various forms of recreation require and without the engagement and rushes of joy and excitement that flow freely during recreation. Pornography and promiscuity have been offered as easy, readily available substitutes to genuine intimacy, committed relationships, marriage, and having and raising families.

These substitutions are sold to people (literally and figuratively) as having specific advantages: microwaves work very quickly compared to real cooking methods and require no skill—anyone can use one; entertainment generally does not require individuals to dedicate time to training or developing any skills, nor does it require getting together or coordinating with others; like entertainment, the substitutions offered in place of intimacy, marriage, and family are offered as things that "spare us the burden" of having to get together with other individuals and coordinate not just a particular activity, but our *lives*.

The relevant question now is whether or not these so-called "advantages" are actually anything of the sort and, moreover, what are their opportunity costs? What is given up for the sake of these alleged "advantages"?

Microwaves require no skill in order to use—anyone can press a few buttons. But is being an unskilled person advantageous? Not hardly. Being able to work a microwave will not make anybody stand out as particularly useful or worthy of greater respect, but the mothers who win baking contests, the bakers who work the local bakeries, and the chefs at the best local restaurants are all admired and deeply appreciated for their skills by the people around them. Skills are often developed out of necessity—various things need to be done and done well. If we get complacent and accept it, microwaves will erode the necessity in our homes of skillful cooking and baking. If we accept what microwaves offer in saving us time and effort and the need for skills, then we will to the same extent be beholden to accept what microwaves offer in terms of what we will eat; microwaves will heat things up in short time, but what comes out can hardly be called a warm meal.

Entertainment, too, promises that we may indulge and luxuriate without the need for any skillful engagement. One show, movie, or video will run into the next in an endless stream, requiring nothing more from us than to pay the electric bill and place ourselves in front of a screen. Such streams do not require friends, nor, generally, any sort of skillful engagement. Indeed, it is often taboo in such "living rooms" to be social and engage with others while a movie is playing or a show is on. To the degree that we accept such entertainment into our lives, we accept a lesser degree of worldly engagement and socializing,

Pornography and promiscuity proposition individuals with the promise of pleasure detached from the requirement of making any promises ourselves. The alleged "advantage" is that they do not require any sort of commitment to other people. In the case of the former, other people can be avoided altogether, in the case of the latter, oneself and others can be treated like fish in a catch-and-release pond. The result of accepting said "advantage," of not committing to others, is that one will be profoundly alone— no matter how frequent the fleeting company of others.

The list of cheap substitutions made readily available to people goes on forever, but the few already mentioned will have made perfectly clear that substitutions are not just cheaply available but also deeply *impoverished* and unsatisfying compared to the real things they are offered in place of. Certainly none of them could be sincerely defended as "even better than the real thing!"

When substitutions show themselves to be impoverished, the richness and poignancy of reality, of what is *real*, is simultaneously revealed. Seeing substitutions as what they are— cheap—primes one's eyes to see what is *real* in all its richness and splendor. Seeing the richness and splendor of the real things makes any return to substitutions sad or even altogether unbearable—and that is a good thing. *One should not settle* for substitutions, and awareness of their nature naturally drives us away from them, in the opposite direction toward what is real.

Indeed, the more we commit ourselves to the real things that we've been offered substitutions for, the more we find ourselves living in *real life*. The fast food, the movies and TV shows, the pornography and one-night stands are all intuitively known to us—and commonly referred to—as *not real*. Everyone knows fast food hardly counts as "real food." Children who cry in the face of some scary thing on TV or in a movie are consoled with the reassurance that what they see on screen is not real. The grotesque inversion of intimacy found in pornography and any cheap charade of intimacy played out in promiscuity hardly resemble real acts of love and are far cries from the reality of intimacy in the context of a loving relationship.

A life filled with cheap substitutions is merely an *imitation of life.*

Grace

GRACE DESCENDS UPON US in two major ways that are immediately recognizable: grace in terms of good will and generosity given where it is undeserved and grace in terms of what we call graceful movement or performance.

The first sort is easy enough to understand: it is an act of grace to bestow something good upon someone despite their not deserving it. We are most familiar with it in terms of divine grace: when God blesses us with wonderful things *despite* our not being worthy of them. But is there a case to be made that the second sort of grace—graceful performance—is also something divine?

It is noteworthy and often duly noted whenever someone moves with grace, sings with grace, or writes or speaks with grace. What is this grace that makes his or her performance so graceful? Why is it so called?

Presumably the grace in a graceful performance is, like the first case of grace, something *given* or *bestowed*. Its borrowing of the namesake would make little sense if there was not something given or bestowed in a graceful performance. What is the nature of this giving, then?

One might say that the performer graces us with her performance, implying that her graceful movement is in some sense a gift to us spectators. But is the performer the one doing the giving? Does a dancer decide to move gracefully on demand, in any and all instances? Does a writer muster all of his intent in order to put most graceful words onto paper? Presumably not; indeed grace often appears to be almost effortless—almost.

Of course much effort goes into practicing one's craft, but grace itself in the context of a performance seems to be an added adornment that descends upon a performance rather than a guaranteed consequence of mastery or something summoned through the exertion of will. Great skill is necessary, of course—if we do not practice a craft, grace will seldom descend upon our performance—but grace is *given*—not accessible or made manifest on demand. Grace itself in this sense is not something practiced, but an adornment received from on high.

We are all gifted—indeed, graced—with talents long before we've done anything to be worthy of them. When we recognize these talents as gifts and cultivate them, we ready ourselves to receive yet a further bestowal of grace: grace upon our performance. In graceful performances, the gifts bestowed on us undeniably double as gifts bestowed upon those who are there to behold the performance, with all of the grace bestowed upon it. The grace evident in one's movements, singing, and words can awe and move and even make believers of those who behold it—indeed, to witness a graceful performance is to witness a performance of grace.

Gratitude

GRATITUDE REQUIRES SOMEONE TO WHOM WE ARE GRATEFUL. Indeed, this is the difference between feeling grateful and feeling fortunate. We cannot feel grateful toward statistical probability or blind luck, only toward someone from whom something was given or granted. On the contrary, to feel lucky or fortunate is to merely feel like the dice landed in our favor despite the odds being against us.

If something is a matter of luck, it may be welcomed with a gleeful cheer or a sigh of relief—but that's about it. When one is grateful, however, the feeling of gratitude extends through time and has much greater depth: given that gratitude requires someone to whom we are grateful, someone from whom we've received something, it it is understood that what was given or granted *didn't have to be*—that what was given could have been withheld—and yet it *was* given, and this signifies benevolence on the part of the giver. Gratitude requires us to recognize such benevolence.

Given the requirement that we recognize benevolence, accompanying gratitude is a sense of *responsibility for* what was given. If your car is in the shop and a neighbor lets you borrow his, it'd be awfully disrespectful to drive it around recklessly or to return it with a quarter-tank of gas. If someone gives or grants us something, it is extremely disrespectful and disappointing to let it go to waste or to just not appreciate it; feeling grateful to someone for something they've given us entails an obligation to make good on what was given, to show our gratitude for what was given by showing that we were—or have subsequently become—worthy of it.

What is more, gratitude seems to give our memories greater endurance—and not just greater endurance, but also greater poignancy and buoyancy. When we are really grateful for something, it means more and tends to stick with us; it doesn't easily sink to the depths of our memory to be forgotten. Rather, it has a buoyancy such that it stays easily accessible, not far beneath the surface of our memories or the surface of our minds. But being really grateful requires *practicing* gratitude. Part of why the things we are grateful for stick with us and remain near the surface of our minds is because in practicing gratitude, we *regularly count our blessings* and *give thanks.* Gratitude put into practice serves as a continual remembering, a continual reminding of all of the blessings and good things we've received and are responsible for.

Indeed, when we practice gratitude and give thanks for our many blessings, we end up being grateful for life itself. We come to find that we are grateful not *just* for these particular things, but also for the fact that life itself is such that these sorts of wonderful things happen, that such things are granted to us. And so finally, it seems to be the case that gratitude orients us toward future blessings—it reinforces that life is full of blessings, and so we ought to keep an eye out. As a result, future blessings and miracles are less likely to pass us by unnoticed.

Hope

AT THE ENTRANCE TO THE UNDERWORLD, Dante encountered the now infamous words: "Abandon hope all ye who enter here." This greeting at the gates of Hell is an instruction to abandon hope, an indication that Hell is a hopeless place, or at least intended to be. In the very least, it is an inscription that implies hopelessness is a defining feature of Hell.

What would it be like to be without hope? When we have hope for anything at all, we can look forward to the *possibility* of something good. We acknowledge at least the possibility—no matter how unlikely it may seem—of something good, and therefore there is something to prepare for, even if its coming to fruition is by no means guaranteed. If there is hope, there is reason to act in anticipation of a future that, though unknown, is pregnant with possibility.

Without hope, without even the bare acknowledgment of any possible possibilities that would later prove our present perseverance worthwhile, perseverance has no point. If there is no hope, why bother? Why try? What is there to prepare for or to strive for?

Of course, our hopes are by no means guaranteed. Often our hopes are dashed, and the old adage instructs us not to get our hopes up for fear of being let down. What we hold up in hope and prepare for in uncertain anticipation often enough eludes us despite our hopeful pursuit—we come to find our hopeful investment of time and effort has been foreclosed upon. And so at our best we hope with humility: we set our eyes on the mountain's peak and set out, seeing many precipices along the way and accepting the potential falls we may take—falls that become greater and greater the higher our hope takes us.

Yet hope carries us onward, and one foot falls in place in front of the other, onward to a destination we aren't guaranteed to arrive at— yet with hope we make our way. Indeed, perhaps the reason that Hell is said to be unwelcoming to hope is because hope—on its own, with nothing else required—is enough to light a way forward with a light that beckons.

Omens

OMENS ARE UNMISTAKABLE—and yet, somehow, they are often also overlooked. To say they
are overlooked is not to deny that they are seen
—rather, it is to say that the omens are seen and
subsequently chalked up as coincidences, dis-
missed as inert and insignificant. While omens
can be shrugged off, the immediate force of
their impact remains jarring nonetheless. The
jarring pause omens give us—the force of their
immediate resonance and the uncanniness of
their being almost unbelievable despite our having just witnessed them—is itself a testament to
their legitimacy and pertinence.

Omens strike us with such force that
they force us to be decisive: either dismiss them
or discern their directive and proceed accordingly. On some occasions, omens take on the
shape of an encouraging wink that we're on the
right path and to proceed with courage; other

times a warning advising us to steer clear or adjust course. Yet other times they appear as a sign of something's significance that we ought to understand and embrace or a reiteration of a lesson we've already learned in theory, but one we've not yet fully brought to bear on our lives.

Omens solicit us; like a knock on the door, at the moment of their arrival they cut through all other commotion and command an immediate precedence, if only for an instant. Whether we choose to answer the knock at the door or ignore it, there was still a knock; so too with omens.

Preserving Mystery

MYSTERIES MATTER: imagine gazing at the night sky on a dark, clear night with all the stars of the Heavens visible. The stars in the night sky hold us in awe—the same, ancient awe known to all of our ancestors.

Now imagine some "know-it-all" character coming up and trying to explain to you that the stars you're gazing at are *"actually," "in fact,"* "balls of burning whatever gas x many lightyears away that will someday, long after we're gone, blah, blah, blah."

Beyond the pretentious claim to have "the answer" to the mystery, there is something about the *attempt* to "pin down" the answer once and for all that is not just pretentious, but perverse and increasingly pervasive. Even if scientists offered some "indisputable" account of what the stars are, the acceptance of such an answer would *rob us* of something much more important than answers: wonder.

Wonder is an intimate encounter with a mystery as timeless as its contemplation is essential and fruitful—despite its being bottomless, inexhaustible, and at times altogether enigmatic. Indeed, wonder's very essence is that it is endless: we wonder *knowing* that the matter will never be completely settled. Yet, in wonder we discover possible and impossible possibilities, and we come face-to-face with the promise of what is altogether unknowable—and yet perennially fruitful to those who wonder.

If there was no mystery surrounding the stars, they would not hold us in awe and sustain our wonder as they do.

But is there more to say about the fruit of mystery and wonder? First it must be said that in wonder, our mind has a chance to wander and discover surprising possibilities in places it hasn't yet ventured, or in places previously visited but now seen anew. Beyond mere possibilities, however, wonder sometimes delivers us over to discoveries that strike as more actual than mere possibilities. The ancient Greek

124

word for truth is *aletheia*, and a literal transla-tion of it would be "un-concealedness." Heideg-ger understood this un-concealedness to be real-ity or things revealing different aspects of them-selves to us at different times. Further, it was understood that this revealing of certain aspects was a simultaneous *concealing* (or at least draw-ing our focus away from) other aspects; in other words, things are always revealing and conceal-ing different aspects of themselves in how they show up to us at different times—and we are awed in part by the seemingly inexhaustible na-ture of reality and things. As time goes on, real-ity proves to us that there was always more to be seen.

We only notice what is there to be seen on different occasions if we don't suppose we've already got the answers all hashed out. In other words, we have to be open to *wondering* about something, even if that something is familiar. To hold ourselves open to wondering about things is to preserve life's many mysteries *as mysteries*.

Acknowledgments

I am blessed to owe a great deal of thanks to a
great number of people:

For their many years of friendship, their
commentary on drafts, and their unwavering
support I am grateful to David Hoinski and Andy
McIntyre. For the very same, as well as his
incredible work on the book's cover—and the
excitement with which he did it—I am grateful to
Eli Maravich.

I am also grateful to my students at West
Virginia Wesleyan College. They have been most
patient and warm during my attempts to live up to
the exemplary teaching I myself was blessed to
have as a student and, what is more, they have
been a wonderful source of inspiration,
encouragement, and indeed hope.

I have been blessed with many great
friends, teachers, professors, mentors, and more.
The lessons learned from them, and sometimes
with them, as well as their many expressions of
belief and support over the years have made all
the difference. They are many in number, and

have differed in role, duration, and effect—yet each of them has been indispensable.